SKATEBOARD STARS

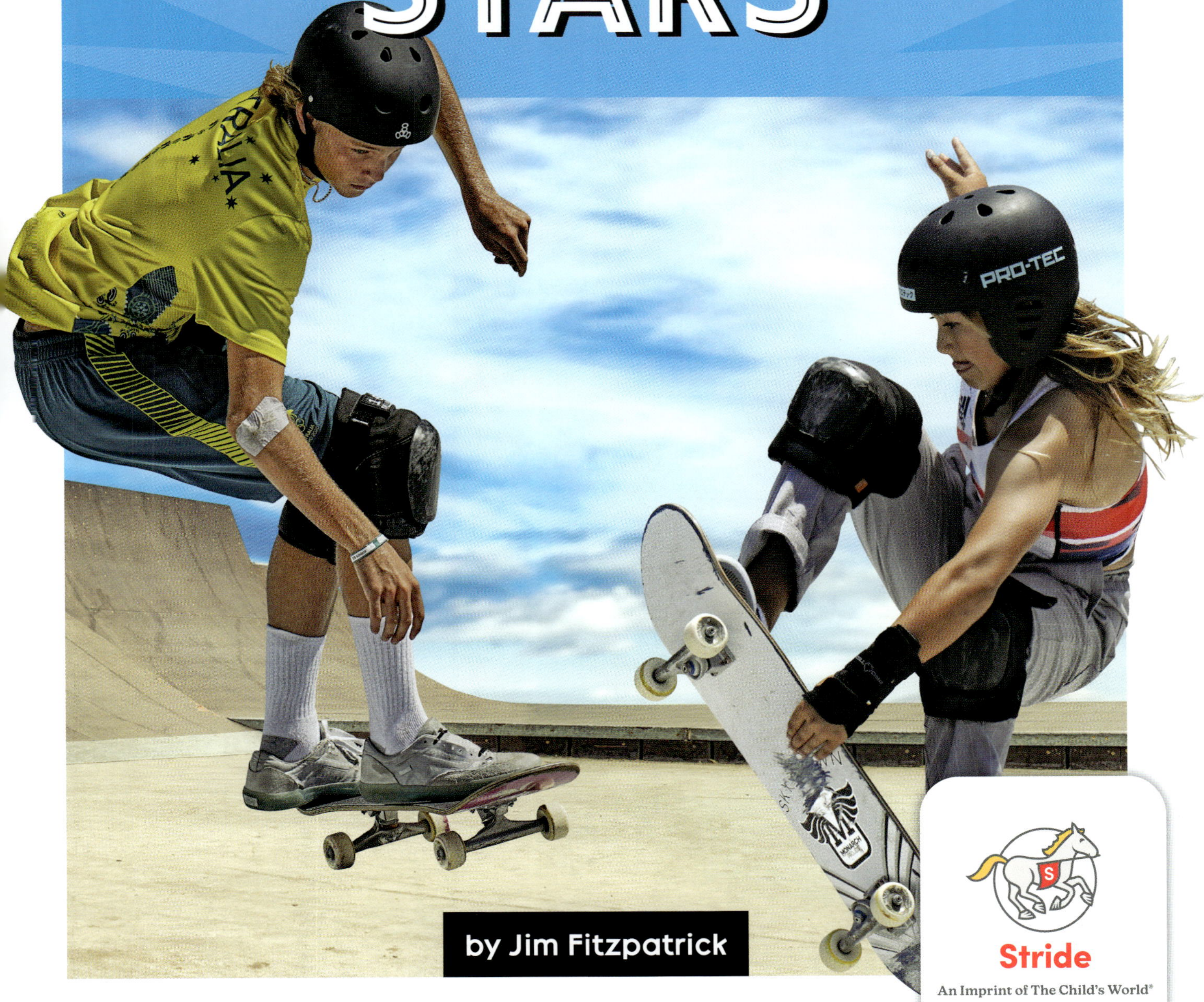

by Jim Fitzpatrick

Stride
An Imprint of The Child's World®
childsworld.com

The Child's World
childsworld.com

Published by The Child's World®
800-599-READ • www.childsworld.com

Photography Credits
Cover, 1: Ulrik Pederson/Nur Photo/AP Images (right); Ben Curtis/AP Images (right).
Interior: AP Photos: Rafiq Maqbool 25, 26, 27. Dreamstime.com: Golubovy 9; Sian Cox 13; A. Ricardo 19. Claudine Gossett: 6, 7, 8. Newscom: Stan Liu/Icon SMI 14; Tony Donaldson/Icon SMI 15; Dan Wozniak 16; S. Bukley 17; Yutaka/AFLO Sport 18; Keizo Mori/UPI 19. Courtesy Kanten Russell: 10, 11. Shutterstock: HurricaneHank 5T; Steve Collender 5B; A. Ricardo 21. Courtesy Skateistan: 24, 28. John Zant: 12.

ISBN Information
9781503858220 (Reinforced Library Binding)
9781503860773 (Portable Document Format)
9781503862135 (Online Multi-user eBook)
9781503863491 (Electronic Publication)

LCCN 2021952382

Printed in the United States of America

TABLE OF CONTENTS

CHAPTER 1

Skateboarding's Story . . . 4

CHAPTER 2

Skateboarding in the Olympics . . . 18

CHAPTER 3

Skateistan Helps Out . . . 24

GLOSSARY . . . 30

THINK ABOUT IT . . . 31

FIND OUT MORE . . . 31

INDEX . . . 32

ABOUT THE AUTHOR . . . 32

CHAPTER 1

SKATEBOARDING'S STORY

Today's skateboarders have fun whenever they grab their skateboard. They skate at skateparks, on ramps, in the streets, or on playgrounds.

Thirty years ago, there were only a few public skateparks in the United States. Now there are more than 4,500. There are thousands more around the world. More than 25 million people around the word are active skateboarders. And in 2021, skateboarding was added to the Olympics for the first time.

Who were some of the skateboarding **legends** that helped the sport become an international hit? Let's meet the heroes of yesteryear and today.

Skateboarders often ride at parks shaped like empty swimming pools.

EARLY WHEELS

The first skateboards were made by attaching the steel wheels from roller skates to wooden boards. Then clay wheels came along, but the ride was still rough. In the late 1970s wheels made of a type of plastic called urethane (YOOR-uh-thayn) changed the sport. The softer wheels let riders do more tricks than ever.

Tommy gets some big air, soaring above a friend after riding up a ramp (in the background). In the earlier days of the sport, many skateboarders did not wear protective gear.

Skateboarding today owes a lot to the many famous skateboarders who led the way.

Tommy Guerrero was part of the famous "Bones Brigade." Formed in Santa Monica, California, the group included more than a dozen top skaters.

In the 1980s, Tommy became a famous "street" skateboarder on the streets of San Francisco. Later, he traveled the world performing before thousands of young skateboarding fans.

Today, Tommy uses his creative powers in his music.

Tommy still skateboards today, but also travels the world as a musician. He always looks back on his skateboarding days with joy.

"Whether I'm skateboarding or playing music, I love the creative part of both," he says. "And with skateboarding or music, it's more fun when you can share the experience with your friends."

Tommy Guerrero was a big **influence** on Ray Barbee. Barbee was also part of the Bones Brigade. He got a lot of attention for videos made of his skateboarding. His picture also appeared in *Thrasher* magazine. Ray even became famous for a trick he mastered—the No Comply.

Here's Ray doing a tailstand back when he was a star skater.

Like Tommy, Ray became a musician. Ray and Tommy often travel and perform together, along with another skateboarder, Chuck Treece. Ray has also become a talented photographer. Some of his work has been featured in museums.

SKATEBOARDING TRICKS

No Comply Combination of a front-side 180 shuv-it (below) combined with stepping off the board with the front foot and then putting it back on the board

Ollie Jumping up while 'popping' the board up off the ground using the rear foot (shown above)

Nollie Jumping up while 'popping' the board up off the ground using the forward foot

Kick Flip Ollie, then flick the nose of the board so it rotates once along its long edge

Pop Shuvit The board rotates 180 degrees, the skateboarder lands with the front foot on the tail of the board, rolling backward.

Kanten Russell remembers being a kid reading about Tommy and Ray in skateboarding magazines. "They always said to skateboard to have fun and enjoy yourself. And that's what I did."

Kanten became a **professional** skateboarder. He **represented** companies as he traveled the world. He put on shows of tricks while riding a skateboard named for him. After a **decade** of traveling, Kanten wanted to do more for the sport he loved.

This is a time-lapse photo showing Kanten doing a trick at a park he designed.

Kanten watches the concrete being poured for a new park in Carlsbad, California.

Today, Kanten designs skateparks. He works with other experts to create safe and fun places for kids to skateboard. The parks feature ramps, curved walls, jumps, and **obstacles**.

Kanten has designed more than 300 skateparks across the United States. After **supervising** the construction, he enjoys skateboarding in each new park. He's the official "tester!"

Like Kanten, Mike Santarossa grew up watching the Bones Brigade. He did most of his skateboarding at an indoor skatepark in Santa Barbara, California. He went on to have a long career in **pro** skateboarding. Mike traveled to Europe and throughout the United States. He also had a board named for him!

Mike wanted to help new skateboarders learn his favorite sport. He became a skateboarding coach. He guides skateboarders of all ages and sizes toward their goal of enjoying skateboarding.

"It's important for skateboarders to learn basic skills first, like how to do kick turns, and carve, and cruise down a sidewalk," explains Mike. "Learning to skateboard is much more than ollies and kickflips and doing **900s**!"

Mike helps a young skater learn to ride over a ramp.

Young skateboarders should wear protection, such as a helmet and knee and wrist guards.

Women have been a key part of skateboarding since the 1970s. Patti McGee, Deanna Calkins, Laura Thornhill, Robin Logan, Ellen O'Neal, Peggy Oki, Judy Oyama, and Wendy Bearer have all been inducted into the Skateboarding Hall of Fame (SHOF).

Patti once rode her board 47 miles (75 km) an hour. That was a women's speed record! In 1988, Cara-Beth Burnside was the first woman on the cover of *Thrasher*, the skateboard magazine.

On a wooden ramp used in skating events, Cara-Beth got some good air!

Other SHOF members include Jen O'Brien, Elissa Steamer, and Mimi Knoop. They have all contributed to the growth of popularity for women and girls skateboarding around the world. They helped women's skateboarding events get added to the Summer X Games in 2003.

Here's Elissa with one of the six medals—including four golds—she won at the X Games.

Tony Hawk is perhaps the most famous skateboarder of all time. Beginning on his older brother's skateboard as a boy in San Diego, California, Tony became known throughout the skateboarding world. He came up with new tricks, soared higher than anyone, and won event after event. He was the first skateboarder to become famous outside of the skating world, too.

Tony does a handstand on the lip of a skate ramp.

Tony and some friends helped create a video game that featured his moves. The game had an big **impact** on skateboarding. Another great skateboarder, Rodney Mullen, says, "Tony's game introduced skateboarding to millions of people who never even considered skateboarding as a possibility."

The video game has developed a **generation** of skateboarders. They have watched the impossible tricks in the video game, but they have also learned regular tricks. SHOF member Kareem Campbell says, "Tony's game took skateboarding to a whole other level."

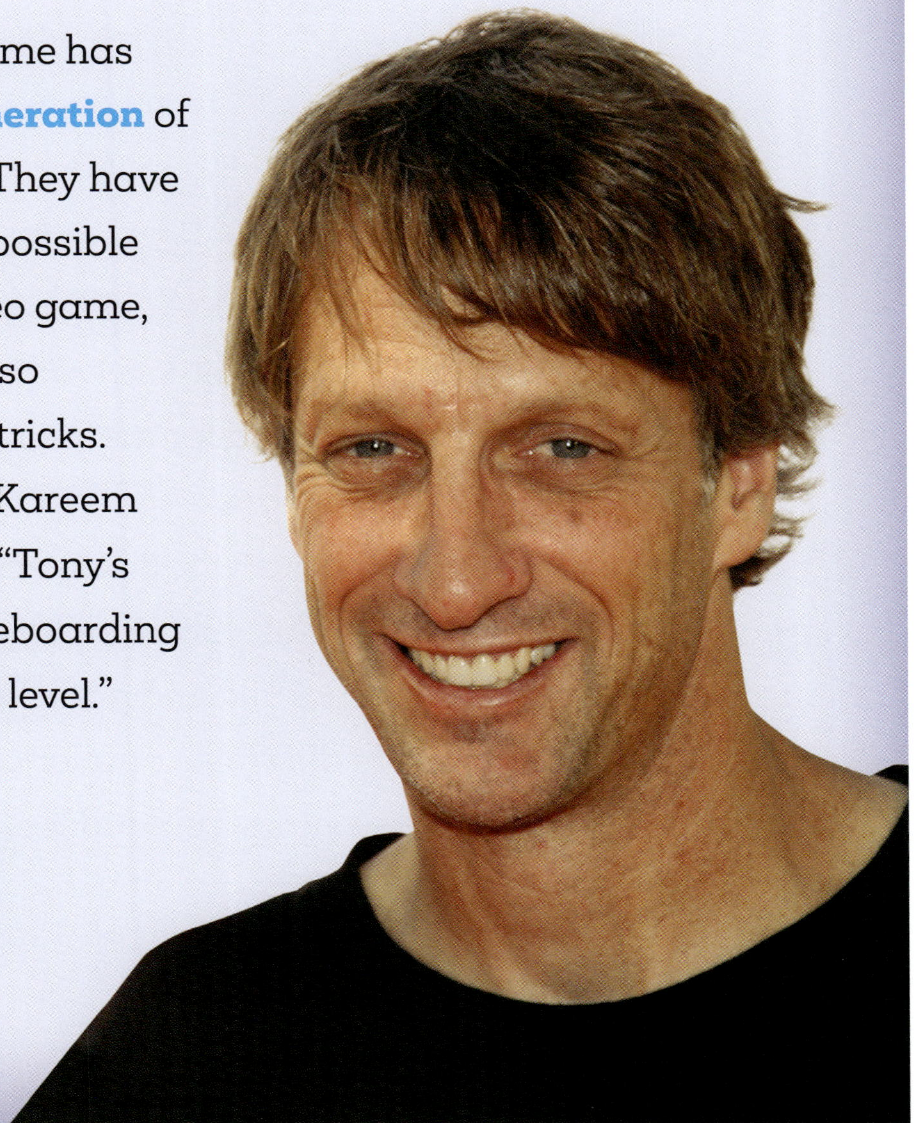

Tony is still a big supporter of skateboarding for young riders.

CHAPTER 2

SKATEBOARDING IN THE OLYMPICS

Thanks to the many skateboarding **pioneers**—and inspired by fans around the world—skateboarding is now an Olympic sport! At the Tokyo Olympics in 2021, skateboarding events were held for men and women in "street" and "park" competitions.

The street event looked like what a skateboarder might find on a city street. The **venue** included ledges and stairways. There were handrails and gaps between other elements. Skateboarders did tricks onto or over all the obstacles, trying to earn points from judges.

The park layout looked like a big, bumpy swimming pool. There were also flat walls and what looked like a volcano in the center of the area. Skateboarders gathered speed along the walls so they could "get air" above the edges of the pool!

Rayssa Leal of Brazil was only 13 when she skated in the Summer Olympics in Tokyo.

Japan's Horigome Yuto made Olympic history by winning the first-ever gold medal in skateboarding. He won the street final when he pulled three awesome tricks in a row. That gave him a winning score of 9.30. Kelvin Hofler from Brazil took the silver medal and Jagger Eaton of the United States won the bronze.

Horigome Yuto was thrilled to win gold in front of his home fans.

The women's street event went to Japan's 13-year-old Momiji Nishiya. She is the youngest person ever to win a gold medal for Japan. The silver medal was captured by Brazil's Rayssa Leal, and the bronze went to Funa Nakayama, another skateboarder from Japan. Finishing less than a point outside the medals in fourth place was American skateboarder Alexis Sloane.

Momiji Nishiya shows off her gold medal, along with a souvenir stuffed animal.

Sakura Yosozumi of Japan won the women's park event when she pulled two **540s**! She carved through the park course with slides and **grinds**. She scored 60.9 points and won her country's third skateboarding medal.

Her teammate, Hiraki Kokona, was only 12 years old, but she won the silver medal. Hiraki was the youngest Olympian to compete in the games over the past 85 years. Another skateboarder, Sky Brown, skateboarding for Great Britain, was third for the bronze medal. Sky was only 13!

Sakura Yosozumi beat the park course with great moves like this one.

Skateboarding for Australia, Keegan Palmer won the gold medal in men's park with two dazzling runs filled with style and skill. He jumped for joy when his winning score was announced! Keegan finished ahead of Brazilian Pedro Barros and American Cory Juneau.

Keegan Palmer couldn't believe it when he saw his gold-medal winning score!

CHAPTER 3

SKATEISTAN HELPS OUT

With skateboarding in the Olympics and with skateboarders all over the world, people are working to bring the sport to even more kids. One group is focusing on places that need safe skateparks for the sport to grow.

In 2007, Oliver ("Ollie") Percovich arrived in Kabul, Afghanistan, with a backpack and two skateboards. He found dozens of children who wanted to use his boards. Kabul was a dangerous place, the site of fighting and war.

Skateistan founder Ollie Percovich

A Skateistan teacher gets ready to teach young Afghan children a new skateboard trick.

But Ollie found a place to skate at the Mekroyan Fountain, a place built by a Russian company in the 1980s.

There, Ollie began skateboarding with boys and girls. As he got to know them and learn what they needed, he was inspired to create a place to help even more kids. While he kept teaching at the Mekroyan Fountain, Ollie created what he called "Skateistan."

A woman in a burka walks past a Skateistan student getting a lesson.

In 2009, Ollie's Skateistan dream came true. An indoor skatepark opened along with a school. Skateistan parks are not just for skateboarding. Children are taught include math, science, and language skills.

Soon after Kabul's Skateistan opened, more than 300 boys and girls were using both the park and school six days a week. Some students learned skateboarding skills in the morning while others attended school. In the afternoon, the groups changed places. Letting girls skate was a very new idea in Afghan culture. Girls are often denied opportunities that boys have.

In 2021, a group called the Taliban took over as the rulers of Afghanistan. The Taliban does not like to give girls such chances. They also closed Skateistan. Some people in Afghanistan are working with Ollie and his team to reopen the skateparks. Ollie hopes to reopen the skatepark soon—but only when it's safe to do so. He knows how much skating can help boys and girls in Afghanistan and in other countries.

Before 2021, Afghan girls got a chance to enjoy skateboarding.

Skateboarders at the South Africa Skateistan await their turns to ride.

The skatepark and school in Kabul were just the beginning of Ollie's work. Today, there are Skateistans in Jordan, Cambodia, Lebanon, and South Africa. At all of the them, boys and girls of all ages learn how to skateboard and get help with school and other parts of their lives.

One thing Ollie has seen is that skateboarding has become very popular with girls. As he explains, "In many places, skateboarding is so new that nobody could say that girls couldn't do it. So what happened? Skateboarding became one of the most popular new sports for girls. Everywhere Skateistan goes, we've been able to introduce girls to skateboarding."

From roller skate wheels to the Bones Brigade . . . from the streets to the Olympics . . . skateboarding is really on a roll!

GLOSSARY

540s spins on a skateboard that include turning one-and-a-half times

900s spins on a skateboard that include turning two-and-a-half times

decade (DEK-ayd) a period of ten years

generation (jen-er-AY-shun) a group of people all born at about the same time

grinds (GRYNDZ) skateboarding tricks in which the underside of the board slides on a rail or the edge of an obstacle

impact (IM-pakt) helping to make a change

influence (IN-floo-ence) having an effect on a person's behavior

legends (LEJ-endz) people who are remembered as being among the greatest in their fields

obstacles (OB-stuh-kulz) things that are placed in your way

pioneers (py-uh-NEERZ) people who came first or who led the way

professional (pro-FESH-uh-null) a person paid to take part in a sport

represented (rep-ree-ZEN-ted) acted in the place of; spoke for

supervising (SOO-per-vy-zing) watching over to make sure something is done correctly

venue (VENN-yoo) name for any place where a sporting event is held

THINK ABOUT IT

Why do you think skateboarding has become such a popular sport?

How do you think music, fashion, and style connect to skateboarding?

Which of the skateboard stars in this book would you most like to skate with? Explain your answer.

FIND OUT MORE

IN THE LIBRARY

Boswell, Betty. *Skateboarding*. Lexington, KY: Apex Publishing, 2022.

Rose, Rachel. *Tony Hawk: Skateboarding Legend*. Minneapolis, MN: Bearport, 2022.

Wiseman, Blaine. *Skateboarding*. Calgary, AB: Weigl, 2021.

ON THE WEB

Visit our website for links about skateboard stars:
childsworld.com/links

Note to Parents, Teachers, and Librarians: We routinely verify our Web links to make sure they are safe and active sites. So encourage your readers to check them out!

INDEX

Barbee, Ray, 8
Barros, Pedro, 23
Bearer, Wendy, 14
Bones Brigade, 6, 8, 29
Brown, Sky, 22
Burnside, Cara-Beth, 14
Calkins, Deanna, 14
early skateboards, 5
Eaton, Jagger, 20
Guerrero, Tommy 6, 7, 8
Hawk, Tony, 16, 17
Hofler, Kevin, 20
Juneau, Cory, 23
Kokona, Hiraki, 22
Leal, Rayssa, 19, 21
Logan, Robin
McGee, Patti, 14
Mullen, Rodney, 15
Nakayama, Funa, 21
Nishiya, Momiji, 21
O'Brien, Jen, 15
Oki, Peggy, 14
Olympics, 18, 20, 21
O'Neal, Ellen, 14
Oyama, Judy, 14
Palmer, Keegan, 23
Percovich, Olliver, 24, 25
Russell, Kanten, 10, 11
Santarossa, Mike, 12
Skateistan, 24, 25, 26, 29
Sloane, Alexis, 21
Steamer, Elissa, 15
Summer X Games, 15
Taliban, 27
Thornhill, Laura, 14
Thrasher magazine, 8
Treece, Chuck, 8
tricks, 9
Yosozumi, Sakura, 22
Yuto, Horigome, 20

ABOUT THE AUTHOR

As a young surfer and skateboarder, JIM FITZPATRICK joined the Makaha Exhibition Team in 1962 and toured Europe to demonstrate skateboarding. Later, he worked to change California laws to provide free public skateboard parks. Jim was also part of USA Skateboarding, which helped get skateboarding into the Olympics. He was also a longtime teacher and principal at a Montessori School.